FRANCESCO PRIMERANO

History of music world.

100thSinatra. 80thPresley. 75ThLennon. 70ThMarley
50thPink Floyd. 50ThDoors. 50thWho. 45ThQueen

Youcanprint *Self-Publishing*

The Legends of Music in their heyday

100 years of Frank Sinatra

80 years of Elvis Presley

John Lennon (75 years after its creation and 35 years after his tragic assassination)

70 years of Bob Marley

The great values and symbols that have left an important mark on our lives

The notes and the pages on the legends of music, from many different colors, shapes and content more inviting, open, they browse, read, love and then close with the hope and the desire to read them again, with the same passion that was initially presented.

Francesco Primerano

Titolo | History of music world
Autore | Francesco Primerano

ISBN | 978-88-93065-50-4

Youcanprint Self-Publishing
Via Roma, 73 – 73039 Tricase (LE) – Italy
www.youcanprint.it
info@youcanprint.it
Facebook: facebook.com/youcanprint.it
Twitter: twitter.com/youcanprintit

TABLE OF CONTENTS

INTRODUCTION
Music Legends Celebration

Artists of music we've had so many throughout history and in the middle of our beloved company, but it has never happened that were recounted all together in a single manual, where anything can be granted, even the unimaginable. The whole world revolves around myths and legends that have made a time of concerts, festivals, records, festivals, embracing all possible genres from Rock to Pop, from Country to Blues, from Soul to Rap, from Swing to Hip hop, from Jazz to Hard Rock, dall'Haevy Metal, punk, grunge to Wave, Reggae by the Black-Music, Electronic Music at the Nu-Metal. This is a good time to enjoy them all, until the last note. In 2015 we want to celebrate the 100th anniversary of Frank Sinatra (The voice), 80 Elvis, Bob Marley 70 and 75 of John Lennon. That same Lennon, 35 years after his tragic murder, wants to be, in this delicious feast, one of the pioneers of our friend Music. A very special year because it wanted to remember the 50 years of Pink Floyd, with their 250 million records sold worldwide, the 50th anniversary of The Doors & The Who and 45-year career of Queen, with their 200 million albums sold planet. E 'own with their new collection, output recently around the world, that you can see at last the return of the fabulous duet Mercury-Jackson who, in more than 30 years since that magical meeting, wants to revive the song "There must be more to life than this ", written by Freddie in 1981 and published in its solo album" Mr. Bad Guy "in 1985. In the course of 2015 will be released also the film" Thriller "in 3D version for joy Fans of Michael Jackson. Speaking of anniversaries, we can also speak of the queen of jazz-blues Billie Holiday that would compiuto100 years as The Voice. You may also remember Jimi Hendrix and Janis Joplin, 45 years after their tragic death. Discs of Beatles and Rolling Stones concerts of Vasco Rossi and Ligabue, live historical groups such as Led Zeppelin and Deep Purple and talents as Bob Marley and Kurt Cobain, they find themselves together in this volume, to celebrate the true essence of the music, the same music that made us love, dream and taste the best nectars of our precious existence. It can be seen, in fact, a fabulous pantheon of Stars to follow, a firmament decided timeless myths, from the class of Frank Sinatra to Rock'n'Roll Elvis Presley, from the myth of John Lennon to that of Freddie Mercury, notes Beatles to those of the Rolling Stones, from the sound of the Queen to the Pink

Floyd, from concerts to those of Vasco Rossi Ligabue, the voice of Michael Jackson with George Michael, by the talent of Bob Marley to the genius of Kurt Cobain, by the determination of the Madonna to the grace of Whitney Houston, from Radiohead's talent to that of the Muses, from Rock to Pop Pelù Jovanotti. This is the legendary world of Music Generation, the true collectors, the skillful acrobats and those who appreciate everything that is music, the music that always governs and accompanies our wonderful lives from curious eternal beauty. This is basically the biggest musical show that we have had the pleasure to know and admire in the paths of our existence, from swing to Sinatra to the masterpieces of Lennon, the Rolling Stones from Rock to Pop Michael Jackson, the legendary Queen to the young Muse, the rocker Vasco

Rossi eternal boy pop / rapper Jovanotti, from reggae of Bob Marley to the grunge Kurt Cobain. You can admire a wonderful flight on the wings of Frank Sinatra, Elvis Presley, John Lennon, Freddie Mercury, Michael Jackson and other myths of world music. It's travel diaries, reflections of the past and of anthologies that reached the top of the charts around the globe. Basically they want to celebrate the myths and legends of music, from Frank Sinatra to Kurt Cobain, the first half of the 900 'to the present day, in all their shades and in all their glory, and you will succeed, touching the heart and the soul of the people who have always admired and followed through with it.

FIRST CHAPTER
Legends of Music
on the border of life and success

See resurrect the true legends of the music world, although on a few essential lines, not every day, and has no price. As was mentioned earlier, in the fabulous 2015 it is to celebrate 100 years of Frank Sinatra and Billie Holiday, the 80 Elvis, Bob Marley 70 and 75 of John Lennon. You also want to celebrate the 50th anniversary of Pink Floyd, The Who and the Doors and 45 years of career Queen, fourth legendary bands that are always kept at the forefront in the world rankings. You can start from any of them, but the important thing is to arrive at the true goal of this festival: to get to all the love and passion for music, accompanied by stunning and beautiful smiles. The Voice can be considered an example of this artistic enthusiasm named "Music Legends". With 63 years of career, 600 million records sold, 1,800 songs recorded in

2000 albums, two Golden Globes, 21 Grammy Awards and two Oscars, Frank Sinatra is considered one of the most prolific and popular artists we had, both in the music scene world that in Hollywood cinema. You want to celebrate its centenary with amazing songs like "My Way", "Strangers in the night", "Night and Day," "Angel Eyes", "One for my baby", who remain still its flagship products. "Live every day as if it were your last" remains one of the main mottos of his long and intense life. But the biggest news is that bubbling "The Voice" is not the only star of the music to be celebrated in 2015: Elvis would have been 80 years old, 75 John Lennon and Bob Marley 70. And 'thanks to the latter that it is popular music genre Caribbean reggae in the world. While we toast their anniversary and their wonderful artistic lives, Freddie Mercury and Michael Jackson recur, to more than 30 years after their great and magical meeting, presenting their song "There must be more to life than this" written in 1981 , published in 85 'in the solo version of "Mr. Bad Guy" and recently added to the new collection of the Queen. They are the ones to be remembered for their unquestionable talent and genius, celebrating the great their fabulous 45-year career with events and projects that will cheer the best fans of Freddie Mercury. During the same year he will also be discussed by Michael Jackson for the theatrical release of the film "Thriller" in 3D and directed by John Landis. In essence, even Michael and Freddie, like other legends, continue to leave footprints music quite exemplary and impeccable, despite their flight to heaven took place some time ago. The different monuments to music (Sinatra, Presley, Lennon, Mercury, Jackson, Cobain, Marley) are the real stars of our existence not only human but also artistic. The turbulent odyssey of Star they live imaginations and magic against power and against the apathy generated by the consumer society. By their example you feel free against conformity and private property, you feel free to sensitize people towards social problems, it feels free through the mist and the madness. Among the many trendy clubs and the habitats of great social impact, there is a fan that is awakened by screams scary or a black roar and there are those who stripped off his clothes wet with sweat Pop, Swing, Jazz, Reggae and Rock. In some remote corner of the street, you can see the curious glances skyward, broken desires that win on thunderous silence and darkness that overtakes the dawn. He is dying to live and to rape the mind, destroying the most real emotions and breaking through boundaries. Triumphs their freedom of speech and the desire to surprise, choosing the best route and breathing their body imprisoned in their "I". While someone sings "nothing is forever in the cold rain of November," it attempts to try to feel the sun what it says today, listening to Freddie Mercury and Michael Jackson. Two artists who have been able to stand, although in a different way, with their exemplary and impeccable talent in the musical and social of all time. Freddie and Michael are reborn again and take the shape and color, even if using a disc of Queen, a song written in 1981 and published exactly 30 years ago solo album Freddie. Two unforgettable protagonists of the limelight pop / contemporary rock come together to give us a

masterpiece of their past. It is a jewel of the 80
'that remains current and lively today. The
sublime voice of Freddie harmoniously binds to
that sweet, sweet Michael, making magic
everything is touched by their charm. Two artists
breed that are second to none, to the point of
being adored and envied around the world. That
their song will never be as successful as the
famous "Thriller" by Michael or as "Bohemian
Rhapsody" Freddie, but surely will touch the
heart and soul of those who appreciate really
good music. Mutations in the seasons of life and
drifting of their passions, the musical legends of
all time have marked their sample with portraits
of themselves in poses are always different and
kidnapped with their prestigious talent of pure
souls of millions all over the world . Their works
are breathing vibrations of pathos and tone of

indifference, tips expressionism and images of deep communication. Oceans of wisdom and eternal presence, large advertising posters, signs of tours, flooding entire cities in search of success deserved and wanted. The lovers of the moon listening to the music of Guns n 'Roses, Metallica, Nirvana, REM, dancing in the middle of the night and enjoying the taste of the soul. You can see that the embrace of the moon and the smile of light can bless the true artists in all their steps. Then you see people who buy their own pride and who throws it out the window, who wakes up with wings of an angel to fly high and who do the walks to learn about the world. There are those who enter the life of another to spread honey in the sun, those who feel the breath of life on him to try new emotions to the music of Amy Winehouse or Tracy Chapman and there are those who finally finds his paradise Rock. They can feel the glow frayed, swirls and hypnotic insane races towards success. In this immensity of pleasure and delirious music you can sing scented breezes, pleading smiles and broken hearts. In the songs of John Lennon, Robert Plant and Lou Reed, you can visit small towns and big dreams with travel through the world of music who plays as if he had something to prove and there are rumors that attempt to get naked, showing a 'honesty that many are contagious. Statements dictated by the heart and soul you can find in the timeless songs of Bob Dylan, Joan Baez, Jimi Hendrix and Janis Joplin. It is these two myths to be remembered 45 years after their tragic loss, remaining anchored in our evenings live blues and rock. Young people seek oblivion in the frantic and Grunge Rock singers like Lou Reed, Jeff Buckley and Kurt Cobain. The night takes possession of souls genuine and true, to the borders of a reality that is becoming increasingly distant between punk rock and beautiful youth, experiencing cocktail of passion and strong emotions. You see guys looking for their way of life and can finally find her in the soul of our friend Rock. Refuse the integrated company, as they did in their time the flower children and hippies: they prefer to live in islands of friendship and pleasure and dive in the delirium and lusts of the night, listening to the Who, the Kinks and Eagles. The signs of the evolution of music is live and perceive in all corners of the city. The commitments in the fight of being and, temptations youth and bestial lust are the main thrusts of these beings full of vigor and hope. A colored people all looking for that deep sense of peace and harmony even to realize a new lease of life: a variety of subjects that prefers bright play, have sex and love to madness. The musical poet plays with our deep emotions: those who closes her eyes in a closet, those who make noise so as not to be overwhelmed by the brutal silence of the night, those who weep and sounds the alarm for help to joy, and those who aspire to something who loses everything, those who struggle to keep a legendary love and those looking for magic in all places to stay alive, because it is the life we are looking for. You see the sweat fixtures pointing a careless singer on stage the night, while his colleague takes a hard decision to not suffer more in this valley of tears. There are those who wake up from dreams in 1000, devouring the world without a specific destination, those who no longer tensions in his memory, and visitors like magic to conquer the stars of life and who wants to be a warrior for every song that can singing. Some people have talent and only one and who is lost in the futility of pain because devoured by ignorance. Some people decide to be a hero and those who choose to live in the simplicity of gestures, telling travelogues in the darkness of the day. There's that fan following Nirvana or Pearl Jam, trying the sweet moans of joy and freedom. Some people can find the time to sit under a blood-red sky and who sings a song by Pink Floyd or Led Zeppelin to dance in the dark of her sadness, but manages to get up eliminating it altogether. Who is the glory to the tune of REM or U2 and those who try despair on their skin singing a song of Jim Morrison and Jeff Buckley. Who finds time for the pain and shame to those who smile, who discovers the ability to break free from nothing and who meets all next to the wheel of dreams. There are those who opens people's wishes and who closes his eyes to happiness. And then there are those who sealed the windows to let the light pass the boredom, listening to Bonnie Tyler, Alanis Morissette or Tina Turner. There's also those seeking the psychedelic rock to the tune of Genesis or Yes, and who kills time listening to Pop Annie Lennox or Whitney Houston. With the Goddess Music is live passions beyond the boundaries of human warmth and thirsty lands,

discovering that some days are better than others and that some nights buy the serenity of always. One can see young people sitting on our star and others confused as of newborn babies; if they see others flying around on the door of sugar, playing the songs of Vasco, Pelù Celentano or Ligabue. There are those who hide their fears to save face, those external gestures deep and sincere to burn the lies of others and who sells his property to get the smiles of Freddie Mercury and Michael Jackson. And then there are those who feed on music to save themselves from the evils of others listening to Queen or Pink Floyd and who gives the latest looks at the wonder of the sound of Jimi Hendrix or Santana.

SECOND CHAPTER
The advent of Music
in the cultural world

Freedom of speech and sexual, the rock'n'roll, the protests against the wars, fashion Pop Rock, the power of the beat generation, race riots, are events that have influenced the musical and artistic culture of each era. The musical phenomenon over the years has seen the rise of new dance clubs and has experienced rapid and dazzling spread of images, colors and great scenery. The music scene of the 70 years 60'e 'attends various changing trends, changing from one type of sound and deep underground to a kind of sound more restless. Assisting reading transgressions, to country-pop ballads, battery-emitting their interesting hallucinations. Lovers of hard sounds and music merciless finally break through the walls of division created by the lack of culture and customs. Free and enlightened inhabitants of the planet are masters of their body and their mind and young people are increasingly impatient with the restrictions. Celebrations of the arts and of what is creative in every individual, frescoes of great artistic seasons of all time, nightly entertainment, are all ingredients that may affect the essence of the music and everything that is going around. Lovers of timeless collections are excited about the rock legends the 60 'and 70' as the Beatles, Beach Boys, Genesis and the Bee Gees. In the corner of some young fans they can see pieces of a youth lived, carefree and electrifying: among that rare material one can see a music outside the lines, following their lifestyles. In their thoughts and in their inner torments glimpsed abandoned rails under the sunsets of joy, hearts always traveling and lying in wait to embrace the day. Some consider the myth of John Lennon the real mirror of his soul and those who worship him for his artistic talents outside the lines. An artist with a capital A, one of the most brilliant and innovative in our musical universe. Is, even today, 35 years after his tragic murder, a social and cultural phenomenon much loved. A man of political and civil that has become an exemplary and impeccable social landscape in the world. At his death (December 8, 1980) began his great legend, and soon became the myth of different musical generations. The great poet of the Beatles has always been the rhythm of an era and the first symbol of the youth revolution. "Imagine", "Power to the people", "Happy Xmas", "Woman", "Give peace a chance", are some of his musical gems. "Anyone can be successful. And if you keep repeating it a lot 'of times, you can have too, "remains one of the mottos of the most interesting of his career. Fans of Lennon hail him and praise him even today, 35 years after his tragic death, considering it the only true God of the music: there are those who dream of finding themselves in the magical island of the artists along with John and those who hope to disappear always from the Planet of the illusions. Some people find the peace to paint everything that is vital to the music of Lennon and there are those who are simply kidnapped. There are artists such as Freddie Mercury, the same Lennon and Michael Jackson they have reached levels considered sufficient to alter the consciousness of generations: those who staged the harmonies of singing, touching the seduction of poetic notes and who sings the sun burning off in the depths. Many musical ideas are already present in the minds of each and are materialized in timeless masterpieces. The things that are being targeted are those that count: the music innovative and cultural impacts that have marked entire periods. Some people develop new styles and who prefers to parodies and covers of other artists, such as deep sequences of dreams and hopes. There are also artists who manage to match the talent with the commitments, tour dates, with their intriguing cravings emerge: Bruce Springsteen, Kurt Cobain, bonovox can be considered as good examples. Poets music give voice to the heart of our thoughts and our souls in celebration. There are examples of original sounds and evocative: you can taste traditional music of tissue grafts purely Rock and you can see contemporary music with more traditional harmonies, songs with guitar and good value with its stirring and profound. There are discs that have traced the furrows marked in the youth scene ever. Posters glimpse of freedom for the individual and savor the brilliant works of bands like Queen, Led Zeppelin, The Beatles, Pink Floyd, Black Sabbath and Deep Purple. Their sound blends music of all kinds and sound aspects of all types and manage to get in a sublime way in our lives already reached by smells and tastes of each country in the world. They notice melodic inspirations that have proved very successful in the entire universe of music; it's travel diaries, reflections of the past and of anthologies that reached the top of the charts around the globe. Different musical ideas begin and end within a minute of notoriety; others, however, persist over time materialized in the best masterpieces of all time. In many songs they tell the spiritual anguish and materials depressed people or those glorious: you can catch stars hanging in the sky and dreams taken away and destroyed by war. Some people ahead of its time spreading the first videoclips of history as Freddie Mercury and there are fans who are immediately kidnapped. There is a fan turbulent and who is freed from all the curses to reach heaven Rock, who is content to watch the show from home and those who prefer to personally go to a concert to exist and to finally say "I was there" . They hear voices that are lost in the wind and you can find various answers and 1000 because of the many songs written for the event by a simple stranger. You see many pages written and scattered on the floor of an empty room but rich in humanity, the room of a young fan full of dreams and hopes. In the drawers of memories and dreams you can be known mermaids and dolphins in search of happiness and even streets that will tell you the routes for the path to prosperity. Feasts Pop, Rock, Blues, Soul, Swing and Jazz, they sing great city to explore beyond the boundaries of reality and drops of life surrounded by the endless beauty. In the various texts of Bruce Springsteen, Bob Dylan, John Lennon or U2 will highlight issues of all kinds, including the political one: "Every system is a cage of anger and injustice because it increases the differences between those in power and those without nothing ". In the songs of Vasco, Pelù, Ligabue, Nomads, Stadium or PFM they are sung queens suburban looking with eyes of anger and looks painted in rainbow colors. There's the fans who lives on the run behind strange and strong orgasms hypocrisy and who opens the door to fight each distorted reality, those who play with words and the speaker alone or with the wind. John Lennon & The Beatles, Led Zeppelin's Robert Plant & Freddie Mercury & The Queen, Ozzy Osbourne & Black Sabbath, The Rolling Stones Mick Jagger, Roger Waters and Pink Floyd, are some of the many pioneers of our musical emotions. Scrutinize details of great value in every musical masterpiece: folkloric elements and dialect, beautiful landscapes, evolutions of timeless talent. Some people leave the city to travel without any goal other than that of big dreams, those of meeting one day David Bowie, Eric Clapton or Leonard Cohen. In the world of music generation, you can see the surprise spells of some places with no name and you see weird pairs of artists in search of success ruthless and difficult to reach. The border of their thoughts will slip on the grass field wet from sweat creative. There are community centers committed to fight the system: those who had anticipated the times as De Andrè, Gaber, Gaetano, Graziani and Baptists and who destroyed them for good, those who survive the defeats as Venditti, Dalla, De Gregori and Fossati and shouting at wind her joie de vivre. Different sounds flood the twisted minds of young fans: pop music of Elton John and the frantic Ozzy Osbourne, the ballad of Michael Jackson and the screaming of Alice Cooper. You perceive tragic visions and exaggerated promises of a reality that other emergency exits !? And then there is the punk of The Clash, Sex Pistols, Ramones, where people meet to dull his senses and give up any notion of survival. Creating projections deafening, the limit of tolerable unbelievable.

They are everywhere invincible personality marked by the need to make scandal.

Hit among the hot music of the latter 50 History of music there are always successes of the Rolling Stones, Beatles, Queen and the Doors. They go through periods of great music and great success. They taste exceptional musical performances of Michael Jackson, Prince, George Michael, Freddie Mercury that send chills even the most demanding critics. It deals with experiments and contamination of any kind and magical spaces of all kinds. Some people drop everything to dissolve into thin air and there are young people who face the music that resonates in the head. These will wait for the colors that really start to flash in the shadows of their soul !? There are those who reach the top of the charts and who knows the strange ways in which darkness desire light: there are discs that have been created and launched with a glittering heart and humble and there are others brought to the forefront with violence and disgust . The bells ring in celebration to the great legends of Rock as Deep Purple, Black Sabbath and Led Zeppelin. Unscrupulous adventurers plunge in performance ever seen, burning traces of our hearts and forever marking the streets of our soul in the storm. Some people oltrapassa the wall and who slams us with great distraction, there are those who feel the need to exist, and who would want to disappear from every face of the planet, marking the paths of humanity: "What the company does not affect the conviction and what man meets destroys it forever. " There is a girl sleeping next to his brother and there's those who shed bitter tears around the world. Sting & the Police, The Bryan Ferry & Roxy Music, Lou Reed & The Velvet Underground: their actions have no other reasons that prosperity, peace and love for all.

CHAPTER THREE
Legends of Rock
from Elvis Presley to Vasco Rossi

Rock music comes to light in the course of the 50' and 60' in the United States and the United Kingdom and has its roots in the blues, country, and especially by the Rock 'n' Roll, Elvis Presley which is considered the undisputed king. The Rock'n'Roll is a rhythm that strays from the ghettos blacks, to become a kind that leads to success great talents as Jerry Lee Lewis, Little Richard, Buddy Holly, Jackie Wilson, Frankie Lymon, Billy Haley, Chuck Berry, Neil Sedaka and many others. But the real gem that stands out more than the others and taking flight before the time is he, Elvis Presley. A real talent that is born in a shack in Mississippi and who performs at school parties with songs typically country. He debuted in 1956 in television shows of great impact, with musical pieces as "Heartbreak Hotel," "Do not Be Cruel" and "Hound Dog". Even

John Lennon praises him with phrases like "Before him there was nothing." "Love me tender", "Loving you," I got stung "," All shook up", "Treat me nice", " Mean Woman Blues ", are some of his greatest hits. "I'm afraid to wake up and find that it was only a dream" it remains one of his most famous phrases and significant. Pure adrenaline, enviably aggressive, sophisticated and brilliant sounds of electric guitars, unsurpassed talent and unique, electrifying voices, are some of the typical ingredients for a succulent dish named Rock. Every aspect, shape, drop or piece of pure Rock gives us the many different colors, sometimes faded, sometimes heated, but still noble and sublime to the point of being considered useful to our mood is not always kind. The variegated colors of the Rock have always that their appeal and their personal beauty, are attractive to those who observe them and scrutinizes them with love and wonder and are essential and true to the purest souls and thinking. Rock Music is the entry, from its inception, in our daily lives, in our homes, in our minds, in our offices, in our dreams, in our cars, in our gestures, in our pockets, in our discussions, in our intimate and sweet

thoughts, and we have met with good humor and wonder, with great passion and at the same time with a little choked up. Now part of us, is silent within us, but lives and if one of us is alive, if he dies is to us, and speaks to us, and grows this curious habit of rock music, which basically want them alive, and he lives with us, lives and opens within us, then continues to live, and expects the best time to grow again, ends with our day, and begins again when we can no longer put her away, can not die, you die and the living. Rock music is always alive and present in us with his notes and best pages because it is impossible to do without it, for over 50 years of history. We should thank our friend often this Rock for his willingness to make himself known, discover, explore, sniff, scrutinize, with its nuances and its variegated colors, smells and tastes. Basically the real music artists, the genes of the sound, the lovers and music experts turn out to be the moral and material wealth of this Rock inviting and appealing. Actually would not exist without them our friend Rock, the Rock that changed decisively and sincere habits of our dull existence. Sometimes we'd love to shout loudly: "How nice it would be if all we became a very good family, even though dispersed and rooted for the various areas of the world, a great family that is united for better or for worse, in victory and in defeats, in joy and in pain, a good group solid and supportive, a great ride of adventures and experiences intensively by special people like us, we who belong to the mythical and fabulous Rock Generation. Rock scene world can meet just about anything: look out divergent ideas, but opinions can be shared by all. They notice the lovers of Rock who listen to their favorite music, which dive into the sublime notes to find the serenity vanished among the various daily problems, that are lost the spell of the sounds found after much soul searching, that are able to embrace the power of their soul to forget the superfluous around us and that win on that boredom invasive decidedly ominous. This is the power that can own only our Rock music, the power to embrace the lost serenity. Musical universe could not miss the true fans and connoisseurs of rock that, after their own myths and idols, they were able to establish groups and clubs dedicated to timeless legends like Queen, Pink Floyd, The Doors, Led Zeppelin, Beatles & Rolling Stones Vasco Rossi & Ligabue. A people still there, present, awake and ready to confrontation: some shares often links and posts dedicated to Pink Floyd rather than those on the Beatles and those who appreciate both, celebrating them everywhere. Pink Floyd have always been as one of the most noble and prestigious Legends of Rock around the world and one of the bands most brilliant in the history of all time. "Wish You Were Here" celebrates its first 40 years of existence wonderful, giving us a special edition in the course of 2015. A record truly impressive and sublime, which is always noticed an attractive balance of rousing music and lyrics amazing. But it was very difficult to keep up with a masterpiece of 1973 as "The Dark Side of the Moon" which is considered one of their most famous albums and sold in the history of rock. The dark side is in fact still a page of history, immortal icon, a disk full of class and fantasy, to the point of being considered the most creative and meaningful in their impeccable career. Besides, almost all their albums, published in 50-year career, representing a true journey of progressive pop entirely harmonious and evocative.

This is the people rock!? A nation of dreamers and great precursors of tomorrow !? There are those who listen to the songs of Nirvana, Led Zeppelin and Guns N 'Roses, and there is the diligent collector who shares links of rare art objects and historical pieces of the Beatles or Rolling Stones. Who wants to remember The Doors, 50 years after their formation, with pictures, videos and stories that represent them in their best performance and who judges them for some of their vulgarity. The Doors remain, even today, one of the most controversial bands and brilliant that we had in the rock scene worldwide. "Strange Days," "Waiting for the Sun" "The Soft Parade", "Morrison Hotel", "LA Woman", " Other Voices "," Full Circle", "An American Prayer ", are some of their most famous records. There are those who follow the legendary Queen, 45 years after their creation. Some people collect everything that concerns them, founding groups and clubs that remember the invincible talent of Freddie Mercury and those who continue to compare them with other bands

without any positive result. The Queen signed
forever true institution of the Rock, yes,

thus, one of the glam-rock formations of the
most successful of these last 50 years of musical
history. Mainly thanks to their sound processed
and pompous, the sublime harmony vocals of
Freddie Mercury, a musical mixture between
glam and hard were always blockbusters. Songs
like "We are the champions", "Bohemian
Rhapsody", "We Will Rock You ", "A kind of
magic", " I want to break free "," Radio ga ga ",
"The show must go on", they signed and topped
the soundtrack of our evenings in the company,
of our parties in harmony and our nectar of life.
And the music of the rock hard and effectively
extended, the dark tones in the higher ones,
unsurpassed voice the eccentric, excessive and
legendary Freddie Mercury. The Artist-rocker

who liked to do things his own way and have fun. If the next day was over all her money would continue to do everything like he had a lot of money, because that's how he used to do, he would go always with a Persian caliph and no one would stop him. He loved to live a full life, and no one could say what he had to do, yes, him, the one who liked to be defining the true queen of the Rock. An unsurpassed talent that returns with his friend Michael Jackson, presenting a song written by him in 1981 and included in his solo album "Mr. Bad Guy '85'. A wonderful surprise for all the fans who find themselves in the new collection of the Queen a jewel of the 80 'duet interpreted by most envied in the world. Of course you are talking about Freddie and Michael, two artists who can not have feared comparison in view Pop Rock world.

But even in the scenario of the Rock Italian you can find a bit of everything. On social and blog dedicated to music, you can meet the followers of Vasco, Pelù or Ligabue and you can know the fans of Gianna Nannini or Berte. There are those who follow with enthusiasm Fossati, Bennato or Celentano and those who remember great talents like Ivan Graziani and Rino Gaetano. There also those who prefer to follow historical groups such as Stadium, PFM, Nomads or Pooh, who loves Litfiba, Fear or the Negrita and who praises genius of bands like Afterhours, Negramaro, CSI or Baustelle. And then there are those who create the pages dedicated to the different performance of Vasco, even putting into question some of his great qualities: someone who loves him and begs him, there are those who are surprised by those who mock and non-believers he retired from great Italian stages or from the extensive music scene. There are those who simply prefer to Ligabue Vasco, and then there are those who consider both of the great rockers to love and to be accepted with the same passion. Vasco Rossi & Ligabue: 2 Emilian Doc, one of Zocca, the other of Correggio, of the same origin, but of different personalities, two undisputed geniuses of rock sound, two different ways of conduct and face the public, two different age, but the same passions, those who were able to engage in a different way and the people rock flawless Italian. Perhaps what unites them who really is just the stage, the stage of the great emotions, the stage of the 1000 occasions and the 1000 personal revenge. Their stage is none other than the altar of their being, their true purpose in life, where they can find their way to purify and recharge, where they can share experiences of love, suffering all sorts of hardships and of each type, which can transmit the real ones and strong emotions that we can only perceive and care. A fantastic world, where they can keep their heads perched in the clouds and feet firmly on the ground, where you can breathe and savor their musical verve, where you show real streams in the middle, where everything is pure adrenaline and nothing but that. A wonderful trip, where is best read the soul of their rock increasingly lively, where anything is possible, even their eternal madness, where everything is amazing respecting one's mind, where everything meets and clashes, and real surreal, magic and poetry, where they can finally show off their true nature adventurous, excessive and evasive, unbridled and unrestrained, succeeding in fabulous aim to please and enrich everyone, absolutely everyone. A real stage in which they themselves are all-encompassing, so they, those that have marked our parties, our love and disaffection, and our nights, our true and dear friendships, our small and big moments of freedom and happiness, so they, our rockers Vasco Rossi & Ligabue. In radio, in various concerts and in several local rock, there are those who want to listen to the historical parts of the legendary Beatles or texts Recent Muse, Green Day, Radiohead, Placebo and Coldplay. There are those who simply prefer the Beatles to the Rolling Stones, making everyone know the neighborhood friends or Facebook. There also those who remember them with images momentous groups and entire pages on Facebook or Youtube. The Beatles were an

English rock band, originally from Liverpool and active on the scene from 1960 to 1970. The four members John Lennon, Paul McCartney, George Harrison and Ringo Starr have marked exemplarily an entire era in music, costumes , in fashion, in the Company and in the history of every day. On October 5, the 62 'they released their very first 45 rpm "Love me do" and in the spring of the following year came out' their long-awaited LP "Please Please Me". From then on we saw them fly high. In fact the Beatles jumped topped the charts and established themselves not only for their music simple and overwhelming, but also for the way they wear certain clothes and wear their hair, imposing somehow their way of being young. From that moment onwards guessed songs
just to break through the universe of music and

social. Soon they became the biggest event of the youth music of all time. And so it was born the Beatlemania, which were infected millions and millions of individuals, to the present day. Their poet John Lennon has established itself in the music world, becoming one of the most brilliant artists and the most loved by the public, so as to be also remembered 35 years after his tragic death. It is also celebrating its 75th anniversary with musical events that will affect all social and 2015. Yes our John would have turned 75 years old, and all of us are interested in knowing what he created with his mind so brilliant and so his soul special. Certainly big business, big things, big institutions and above all the great works of music, bringing us so far away from us breathe great emotions.

FOURTH CHAPTER
The magical sounds
of Rock Generation

Artists Rock should merit the special prize of the beauty of mind: transmit with their essence and their song the healthy vein of freedom the world has always dreamed, emit with their strong and gentle sound of the joy of life that many would like to own. Their delightful and lovable presence manages to cheer our warm days and make all that magic can occur in our life paths hard and intense. Among the fabulous notes of Vasco Rossi, Ligabue, Queen, Pink Floyd, The Beatles and other legends of Rock, you can grab fragrant breezes, fever smoke who lives in the bodies of rebels and smiles pleading decent people. You can feel the grin jungle music beyond the sea and sky. Inside the sound of timeless songs, there may be red from the wine roads, a good vintage wine, and also the clown smiling and gives smiles, young brisk singing and dancing in the day and in the dark, glowing embers and hugs turbulent in magical lands, open windows and unmade beds. On the banks of their musical soul can be seen with surprise the eyes of the heart imprisoned in anything of our absences and essences. Listening to the brilliant Rock and surreal, it goes beyond the voice and in the sounds of our hearts. In various passages he tells how the spirit of the people can buy music dreams offended by the corridors of power and suck nectar of innocent lives and attractive. Also you can find sparks of pure youth and festive and eternal paths towards hope. Patti Smith, the true and undisputed poet of Rock. Janis Joplin, the blues-woman par excellence. Tina Turner, the woman Rock a great determination. Bonnie Tyler, the Artist Pop-Rock enviable qualities and scratching. Alanis

Morissette Princess of Rock '90s: the great shining star of the Rock in the immense depths of freedom and vanity, on the edge of the mad dash for success. Their music turns on the character and the greatest dreams. Their fantastic sounds spread fleeting flowers of these words and concepts written on the walls. They tell shreds of memories faded by rain light, reddish glow of a sunset bold, unprecedented happiness of emeralds, crystals of visions and images of enviable energy, rebellious spirits and free, devouring news and dreams of poets timeless. Leonard Cohen, Cat Stevens, Bruce Springsteen, Jeff Buckley, Bob Dylan, Neil Young, Frank Zappa: poets and true pioneers of the Rock. In their sonnets there is also the purity of mirrors that reflect furtive caresses and you can see nostalgia without hope, adrenaline and vertigo without memory, endless shows of great glory, ties loose and roads combined with the tenacity of music that sets them apart, and then walls collapsing unscrupulously, extinguishing the eyes of young stalwart and vibrant. Lou Reed & The Velvet Underground, Mike Oldfield, Tom Petty, Tim Buckley, Meat Loaf, The Cult, The Scorpions in their lyrics speaking of the time, a little time or a long period of lives visceral, the same time, of our precious time, time that takes care of the wounds of our soul. Alice Cooper, Ozzy Osbourne, Eric Clapton, Jim Hendrix, Santana, Kurt Cobain: in their stories told there may be collapsed castles and temples have been raised, the rooms and the vast prairies of the soul and the heart, burning eyes or silver smiling at our existence. You may find traces of heaven in our minds that run furious and lost into the unknown, lighting universes and colors never explored. It is wide open to life the twisted minds and tired of a world to discover and savor. They tell sublime paths in gardens, in the humid nights and cold, sweet and intoxicating places, in the infinite labyrinth of consciousness, and then sing streams open and healthy, young souls and spigliate towards the road to success and into the realm of freedom . In reality it is a Fabulous world that take your breath away !? Rock the world of Jim Morrison, Freddie Mercury, John Lennon among their lawns music floating white horses and race and it denotes the breath of our desire always ready to live every moment. Between songs and notes of Queen, Pink Floyd, the Beatles, the Doors, Nirvana, you can see small lamps that illuminate our freedoms, vivid landscapes and colorful ghosts of lives that are canceled, roads impossible to travel, huge roses of blood , still sweet and sincere. And then they sing with great fervor eternal caravans dolphin smiling, fabulous places among the brave clouds, full lips and never nervous, the golden hair or steel of a child lively and lovely. In view Rock overlook punk or dark quite ingenious and original: The Cure, Sex Pistols, The Clash, Ramones. Discussion of issues of all kinds are exposed and pieces of life in the various musical poems of these genes of Rock: the white robes and holding of an angel, the old and new glories of our day, the dew drops of spirits in the storm, the kiss gush between subjects that you love, kissing the trees in the twilight, the powdered clowns in the streets of the country, the happiness of the sun in the paths of young brides and the bloody light of dawn. Among the works they will run through Rock themes of all kinds, content thorny and burning and you live shivers of pleasure. Among the songs of Guns N 'Roses, Nirvana, Pearl Jam, Metallica, Cranberries, Smashing Pumpkins, Sound Garden, tell the arrows of rice and cried, birds glorious soaring, red and fiery spirits of people polite , the rolling green poplars, the clear sky of October and November rain "Novenber rain". Between the words and the traces of their musical poems, is living the passions of the woods, the white violets on the faces suspended, villages full of harmony and long looks that explore the night of stars. Music in the clouds one can see the souls playing in the blue river, the girl of the wind that runs happily in the meadow of flowers, you can collect colorful shells and cymbals crystal, and can also beat the hearts of ducks serene. You can discover joyful children who bring silk sheets, white doves that paddle through the waters of the lake and white horses in the green hills of a timeless landscape. uncertain and gloomy. The pioneers of rock strike again with their stories of life and hope. You sing the sweetness of dusk, leaves stained moon in the night blue, orange blossom gleeful, south winds, the water of the river full of sun and sunsets fishing and sugar. Among the notes of Genesis, REM, the Who, the Kinks, Yes, Eagles, AC / DC, you can enjoy years of favorable skilled heroes, sincere tears of mothers suspended, blue flames of young hopes, loves legendary, endless talents, or more days unripe days and the lake shimmering poetry and imagination. You can meet the dreams of gentle swans who breathe clean air and that feed on white light, you can see silk trees that greet consciousness. There is the beautiful night that crosses paths with clean bird catches the worm, buyers pride with glowing embers of a bright red and who grasps suspended tears into the soul. Between songs and notes Jefferson Airplaine, Nazareth, Emerson Lake & Palmer, Boston Cream, Supertramp, you can give birth tears and stars between stones and rocks, you can enjoy endless sweetness and old records, tunnel of piety and great despair, jukebox of joy and timeless musical pearls. There are those who gives words of love and unbridled passions and those external interesting stories to tell: "Each of us has a story to tell or Rock you can show off, whatever age you can wear. Each of us has a life of his attractive, stimulating, exciting, but always personal and unique to the point of being proud. Each of us is special in its noble or praiseworthy enterprises Rock, but also in its delicious and small gestures. "And 'changed the Music Rock over the years !? Radios cheering and smiling in the sun. There are artists punk, jazz and blues that are made of deep strolls in the dark side of life and there are those who seek the love and desire at all costs. Deep Purple, Chicago, Bee Gees, Beach Boys, The Byrds, The Scorpions: there are regular Rockers or out of time, others who think and sing addressing the past. Some people look back with nostalgia and those watching the future with joy "Yesterday", and those who think that the time always wins, overwhelming us with its hopes and its illusions. There are those who like a healthy precursor of tomorrow and those who like a simple homesick. There are those who embrace the time and who escapes, there are those who do not fear the future and is ready to enjoy it with both hands as it always has for its fantastic rock past. There are those who feel that the years fly and who caresses them with good humor, who tries to collect and capture the 20 years with an enthusiasm rock a little warm but pleasant, taking advantage of their generosity and those looking very firmly grasp the ' present moment "Time". You can find the artist Rock thinks that even the children defenseless, those children to love and care for, those same children who, for the simple fact of being such, they have the clear right to live in serene land where you can always smile and be followed in the most exemplary for all. This is the world we have created, what we have or what we invaded devastated !? This is the world of rock'n'roll !? from which you can extrapolate secret harmonies, spells endless rainy days heartless, evil and good answers to life, lights eyes vigilant, sensations and pleasures of all time !? Green Day, Radiohead, Placebo, Blur, Skunk Anansie, Lenny Kravitz Rock are other actors in a more innovative, a real explosion of ideas and emotions, a mixture of different shades and effective, a Wave Outside the Lines, in substance a new artistic style and sound, a new way to express the great musical show. Listening to these sounds soft and deep enough to let go and take to the mad joy !? It would be enough to look soulless nights grabbing the unknown heart !? Find enough angels happy, souls in full, eyes special and full of magic, yuppies in action and always in the game !? Would be enough to find reflections of light and joy, the sea in our veins and try sailors and sellers of happiness !? U2, Kiss, Van Halen, Aerosmith, Alan Parsons Project are other pioneers of our brother Rock. There are situations and precious stories that are told in poems rock of all time: describes the soft banks of the lake, the full moon in the emptiness of life, and then the home of dolphins smiling welcoming new friends. Overlook the various human frailties without space, the eternal departures and landings made by now. It can see finally a Rock of hope and light ¡? Among the pearls music of Pink Floyd, Led Zeppelin, Beatles & Rolling Stones, describing the best 50-year history of the Rock, are sung border towns, ecstasy and omnipotence, the stars of the sea crossing ' smell of the river and pockets of social problems. There are refugees and traffickers want, shots of real joy, the first fruits of the dawn, travelers traveling, zoom images love, to open windows and blind love. Rock and around !? When someone speaks of pure Rock, others respond with even folk songs, and there are those who respond with soul songs, with lyrics jazz, blues songs, with notes grunge and glam sounds. Simon & Garfunkel, Sting, Bryan Ferry & Roxy Music, Mark Knopfler & Dire Straits, are some of the great protagonists of our precious emotions Rock, those same emotions that you can not understand or explain, but you splash to live intensely. Among these feelings Rock overlook the jesters of our heart, the tea leaves, the starry heavens and the lovers of the moon, the moon of October, dreams without age and various scars of the soul. You see even rising Artists and craftsmen of feelings, scenarios of the past, sailors with faces to crack, sniffing serene worlds of poetry, yes, that's right, true and delightful poems rock, nothing more than that.

In the music scene are certainly present different types of fans or those affected by the contagion of pleasant Rock Generation. In various clubs and rock concerts are crazy games without poetry, you see out the fire of love, you see young people on the streets free and vast meadows: there are those who pay the bitter price of happiness and who is lost in despair of age. Some people live and die of pleasure and who relishes lust and adrenaline in its purest form. You can find the young schoolboy who plunges in the notes of his favorite music, compared with all that is vital and healthy and who thinks everyone should give meaning to their existence, by sliding the displeasure between the notes that count always rock . Some come to light to perform and be always trying to dispose of trouble and sorrow, we are fellow insomnia shared in the good times and bad, and the party that wants to face challenges electrifying. Some people try to revive the seasons of love or who simply finds the love in every season of the soul. There are fires that flare Rock and never go out, those who love and those dirty scratches of pure emotions, who was struck by the joy of others, trying to smooth the edges of your twisted character. Some people prefer to follow a glorious band like Pink Floyd, Beatles & Rolling Stones rather than a political party unnecessary and tedious. Some believe that being children of the rock makes us fathers of large and inviting ideas and there's the guy who asked about the future and not finding adequate responses mingles among the known rock in order to realize those desires that no one would have dreamed to follow. Some think that the rock faces shrouded in mystery are the most intriguing of those who wrap themselves in the banality of their appearance. Some like the events and news rock which are not trivial, they do stravivere yet another youth and who know how to excite most of the past. There are those who admit to having always scrutinized and praised the positive and all the pleasant qualities of the Rock, or he would have continued to hate the whole of humanity and who considers the human being the worst part of a monkey insignificant. There are those who appreciate people for what they are in their positivity trying not to denigrate them for what they are not. Some think of finding between notes Rock those smiles that had been stolen from his loved ones enemies and those seeking to taste morsels of happiness that were lost along the way. Rock the universe you can meet also those guys who try in every way to satisfy those emotions that had died during a hellish day or in a matter of hours spent in nothing. Some people try to enjoy those moments of freedom he had lost in a matter of hours of stress and boredom and who can sing thoughts and words dealing with Ms. Liberty. There are others who still believe in the great value of freedom in all its forms and all the people rock needs to believe again. Some people try disgust towards the disciplines imposed by others, only for their taste of power. Some people believe that the rocker is born free rejecting the hypocrisy and the blackmail of those who govern, who can find true freedom by living the rock and shamelessly showing strengths, weaknesses and character and then you realize that freedom who was looking for was right around the corner or in the drawer of our soul always ready to help us out kind and gentle. Some people try to kill boredom and who you contaminate and grasping tentacles of unhappiness. There are those who, in these huge empty, try to find the fullness of their lives, and those seeking to fill the small voids in the best way, listening to everything that is full and vital. Some people can find himself consider ourselves even more, but it is only a true illusion or the achievement of a desired pleasure always !? You can meet those chasing lives and pleasures that are not approved at the mass and those who think that the best dream is to continue doing everything we like to do and create with the ideas Rock. There are those who find an old friend rocker, but not a new treasure, some people think you have met the true love, but it was not what he wanted and those who consider love as a wonderful adventure in which to run without thinking in search of conquests Rock increasingly intriguing. Some people think that rock music can make us nourish its nectars best, those of a freedom that only she can give us with its warm welcome, that salutary hospitality that only we know adventurers sniff. Some believe that real music is to try and flush out even and especially in our dear nature, where you may find something very large and indefinable and those who think that music has the power to make us feed of pure freedom and wealth interior, when we feel gloomy and poor intimately. Some consider the art of music as an invention for which he must live, one of the best forms of expression on the earth, creating as catharsis, the one faith, the only lifeline in a society that It is drifting and without it the people rock would have no reason to exist. There are those who believes the Lady Music as a bridge between people and a good way to grasp the hidden rock universe: this form of expression allows us to unravel the mysteries that elude us and better understand the world and also It helps us to shape a certain idea of happiness and pigs often in harmony and peace and the need arises disproportionate to know to better understand all the sounds around us. Among these young people full of hope, you can breathe paranoia and panic, lust and gusts of wind, ghosts in the pockets emptied out of nothing and the eternal love with the moon. You notice that the bells ring in celebration, oceans of magic and beauty of spirit, soul and the sweet flow of love in the folds. Among the musical souls you can also find those who want to capture the moments of glory and the best years of his life in historical images of photos as delicious pieces of life.

FIFTH CHAPTER
Legends of music 80' and 90'

In the grand spectacle of the 80'and 90' are lived endless emotions and so many experiences that have changed the history of humanity: those who risk slipping on the grass of the fields bordering the malaise, who gets carried away by falsehood and hypocrisy, who loses his senses, who seeks out those precious pieces that are missing to complete the great puzzle of his sweaty youth, those who try to anticipate the times, those who manage to survive the defeats and shouting to the wind his damn joy of living between the magical notes musical and artistic works of all time. Acts of common courtesy that mark the days of the existence and the glorious 80 'and 90' are most welcome to posterity: who walks on a rainbow and who runs on the edge of a pop song or a rock song. Among the commitments, the sacrifices, the many difficulties and the dramatic events of those years, you can find the murder of John Lennon, the liberation of women, the fight against all forms of racism, the tragic death of Rino Gaetano, l ' education of children to peace and respect, the defeat of hate and poverty, the fall of the Berlin Wall, the untimely death of Kurt Cobain. All historical events and symbols that have changed time and achievable goals through the joys of music, culture and art of those years. The focus of the artistic talents of Duran Duran & Spandau Ballet, photos of Michael Jackson kissing Madonna, festivals Jovanotti dedicated to Vasco Rossi, the Queen always at the top of the charts, are traces of a youth exhilarating and true, as the wings of our desire, flying and crossing roads to success, capturing everything that can be eaten in those years. The key that opens the door to happiness and genuine ray of sunshine are the most genuine aspirations who aspires to the infinite richness of the soul artists such as Michael Jackson and Freddie Mercury. It all makes sense and taste in those years: gatherings of old stars and amateurs, discs of value appeared on the shelves of shops, songs sung and played in electronic and pop-country. In the skies of the legendary 90 years 80'e 'they will uncover artistic skills of sounds that flood the mind of the listener: you notice between the various fan of Madonna & Cindy Lauper, eyes twinkling subjects adorable and soap bubbles flying on their faces. Enjoy the fruits of artistic work of Prince & Michael Jackson allowed to surf on the crest of the wave, enjoying success in relationships of all kinds, to meet cultural needs and to have a special affinity with the whole universe. Humors and grinte agents, rare talents and special qualities distinguish personalities and artists such as Cindy Lauper, Annie Lennox, Barbra Streisand, Laura Branigan and Jennifer Rush. Who captures with great style the substance of pop music 80 years 'in its fullness and who dives to the tune rock 90s'. The vital essence of Duran Duran is disarming to the point of not fearing the other groups in vogue in those years as Spandau Ballet, A-ha, Eurythmics, Tears for Fears and Roxette. There are those who embrace the artistic qualities of Michael Jackson, Boy George, Prince and George Michael, who tasted with pleasure the performance of Madonna and Grace Jones, who embrace fully the musical notes of U2 and who tears up the poster of the Pope as Seaned o'Connor. It can be argued with great enthusiasm that our great musical past has been signed in an exemplary manner by these decades of great value. The time to live with precious friends walking by the sea of memory, seizing power and beauty of youth: exploring the successes of Depeche Mode and Ultravox, listening to the music of Talking Heads or Smith, playing under the orange blossom and diving on the notes Diana Ross and Donna Summer, artists who were able to impose as early as the late 70'. Music brilliant, engaging performances and magical atmosphere in which they were created with the best songs of all time, are other ingredients typical of those tumultuous years. Songs that leave a mark, and that fascinate many fans and music fans are the true strength of that time, becoming in time the true symbols of those decades and today is a leader in the following years as pillars of other generations.

There are those who try to slip into their world and in their songs and who escapes the trappings to embrace something more vital and different. The true light years 80'e 90 'does not disappear completely in the 2000s, indeed is felt more than ever with specific programs and concerts in their honor. There are those who locates the best times to break through and those who want to spend a few moments of serenity to the tune of Tozzi, Raf, Vasco, Stadium or Sugar. Remember legendary atmosphere in privileged areas and specialties of all kinds savor from paninari of those years: there are young people who are deer on the beach and others singing a song by U2 on the riverbank. Acts of value that the people of the years 80'riesce to demonstrate, remain etched in the minds of each of us. Some people live on the waves of youth without disturbing the peace of twenty years and those who collect posters with images of an era that will always be remembered with longing and affection: immemorial seasons, new generations in fire, pleasant memories and legendary diving in roads returning to the mind as sublime paths of the soul. The mere sound of the band returns the joy in the hearts of rebels paninari in action: those who act ahead of time and who do not pass up the opportunity of a lifetime. You can see the floors soul wet from the genius mind of bands born in those years of glory and you can taste fires burning out of control. This is the wonderful world of 90 years 80'e '!? where new generations cheering and wonderful travel on oceans of adventure and fun and poetic notes on artists such as U2, The Police, REM and Nirvana !? A radiant smile always always leads to great achievements in music of that time, if the vital energies are spent with a healthy curiosity in a surprising social activity. Some people try the unique sensations of freedom, who dives on attractive notes of Depeche Mode, Soft Cell and New Order and who finds himself in the real and tragic events related to the history of those times. The places of the mind and of the heart can make wonderful trips in those delicious decades, where everything costs many smiles and a sip of madness. Some people prefer living breathing culture and music of the 80 'and who is lost in a night of nothing stupid singing a song by Radiohead, Nirvana or Skunk Anansie, brilliant examples of the 90'. They occur so the two fantastic decades: the joy of making a kind act, the energies of musical passion transmitted by Duran Duran and

Spandau Ballet, the scent of happiness falling like drops on the skin of great artists like Kurt Cobain and Axl Rose, open views towards big dreams and new musical achievements. These unforgettable pleasures of life plus the sublime sensations of valuable people and original sounds of bands like Talk Talk, Ultravox, Soft Cell, A-ha and New order. Then they see fans peering from the windows, autograph on album covers and the desire to emerge. There is something that does not need much explanation in those years: analysis of music and record companies, many masterpieces that have made a mark in the history of music and art, encouraging comments and suggestions sound of all kinds, an endless series of vibrations and items that have caught the sign, fragments of timeless works and peace movements. Artistic careers that have had some originality see emergence of the stars of that time as Whitney Houston, Bonnie Tyler, Tracy Chapman, Kate Bush, Janet Jackson, Gianna Nannini and Loredana Berte; their adolescence found in music a sign of their conflict with life and with their true chance. They will retrace their paths, their lives uphill, their popularity and their profits. The musical and artistic events of all kinds have grown enormously and there is a process of composing many masterpieces: concerts and shows that have made the history of music license plate 80'e 90 years'. The introduction of CDs and music videos in the world trade and in the various schedules is a shot in the arm to the music industry. Remember Live Aid in 1985 in two places very significant as Wembley Stadium in London and JFK Stadium in

Philadelphia. Grace Jones, Debbie Harry, Bonnie Tyler are some music artists of once-glorious unforgettable performances that have marked every artistic line to find in the heart of the city and allow to grab a few pieces of sky. There are issues that are profound and sublime handling and distribution in the songs of that time: no need to look more to see the wounds of the soul, there is the flame of passion that spreads faster in the breeze our thoughts, there are paths of freedom which are close to the happiness of our dreams. In the garden of the eccentricity will have the real stars of the pop scene, without ever losing the characteristics of the best talents timeless. This raises new frontiers and every new album introduces a new facet of the youth. There are those who flies on the wings of happiness listening to the thoughts and words that have left an indelible mark in the world and someone pulls out of the closet musical historical pieces of those who have changed the history of two decades. You notice the desire to bite people, the urge to eat the eyes of others, the special visions of famous characters, the last drops of blood that save the Rock'n'Roll as Guns N 'Roses and Nirvana, the abundance of goods materials and all that is vital and positive. Every minute of the 80 'and 90' is considered the most beautiful, the most real, the most artistic, the more alive than others. Some people crave tomorrow, some people in the street dance, singing a song of Michael Jackson or Madonna and who goes on show to steal all the limelight. The various sequences of the two decades are symbolized by introspective artists of great value to effective representation of timeless images: meticulous research work and documents of great interest to anyone who wants to understand what lies behind the success of that time. Duran Duran, Spandau Ballet, Depeche Mode, U2, Ah-has conquered the musical world with music and images that have made history. In those hot and amazing glory years, young punk paninari and girls think and hope strongly to be the center of the world, but can not understand what the music genius of that time was the center of their thoughts. They need wonder to fill a void, but the surprise for Music license plate 80 'is not enough to be able to honestly fill. In any music stars they notice considerable talents: artistic and literary creativity are closely linked by their talent without control. Every drop of fate kisses the conscience of artists in trouble, because they represent the souls of true desire to succeed always. Who leaves the city for traveling without a goal and who often chooses the way of the great dreams Rock, rejecting that of small torments. Artists in search of success ruthless and unjust are the first to be swallowed without great success: who collects the needs of entire communities and those who wasted artistic unscrupulously. Magical atmosphere of beautiful places to admire and praise are always the goals of those who know how to dream pop and rock music with their eyes open. There are young bands that sparked so much to gain a bit of notoriety, but are never the height of rock icons that have left an indelible mark and there are others with talent and ability insurmountable. Who sings the first sparrows spring at heart of beautiful places and people running towards the sea of joy. The shadow of pop stretches as the sun sinks into the sea of rock to give light to the emotions of a new life. The storm that rages in the eyes of a child acquires shades of blue and red spanning the heart and soul of who really is in the roaring 80s 'and 90': there are those who continually looks attractive rates joy, who He lives in underwater worlds by boredom and listener of good music to be impressed by the positive influences of those times.

The best dreams are certainly those that can be made especially in difficult terrain and trails and roads easy to go, otherwise you have fun in desire them!? And finally those famous and delicious dreams we had chased always have been able to realize in the best way. Those sounds sublime and sweet that we have heard of the wonderful notes of Legends timeless, nothing more than the magical world of music, the same music that made us dream, love, know and enjoy the best nectars of our existence and that we He has taught us once again that, whatever happens, the show must go on.

♪ ♫ The Show must go on ...

♪ ♫ The Music must go on ....

♪ ♫ The Life must go on .....

Frank Sinatra, Elvis Presley, John Lennon, Bob Marley, Freddie Mercury, Michael Jackson, Kurt Cobain, Pink Floyd, Queen, Beatles, Rolling Stones, Vasco Rossi, Ligabue and other legends of the music chanted in an exemplary manner the true and deep essence of our lives.

Many thanks to all
Francesco Primerano

The pages and notes on Legends of Music, of various tints, shapes and content more inviting, open, they browse, read, scrutinize, they love and then close with the hope and the desire to reread them again with the same passion that he had initially presented.
(F.Primerano)

Finito di stampare nel mese di Settembre 2015
per conto di Youcanprint *Self - Publishing*

www.ingramcontent.com/pod-product-compliance
Lightning Source LLC
LaVergne TN
LVHW091556170726
843492LV00007B/2161